Talented Animals

A CHAPTER BOOK

BY MARY PACKARD

SCHOLASTIC INC.

New York Toronto London Auckland Sydney
Mexico City New Delhi Hong Kong Buenos Aires

For Justin and Kate

ACKNOWLEDGMENTS

The author would like to thank all those who gave their time and knowledge
to help with this book: Lou Ann Best, Bowman Hastie, Anne Gordon,
Dr. Penny Patterson, Dr. Ronald Cohn, and Lorraine Slater of the Gorilla Foundation,
Richard Lair, and Dave Ferris of the Asian Elephant Art and Conservation Project

ISBN 0-516-24461-2

12 11 10 9 8 7 6 5 4 3 2   3 4 5 6 7 8/0

Printed in the U.S.A.   61

First Scholastic book club printing, November 2003

CONTENTS

INTRODUCTION

Get ready to meet a group of amazing animals. Most have fur, a few have trunks, and one has a bushy tail. They come in different colors, shapes, and sizes. They share one thing in common, though. They all have a special **talent** that sets them apart from other animals.

Twiggy the squirrel can water-ski around a pool in her toy boat. Tillie the dog makes paintings, while Koko the gorilla makes up words to songs. Bird the elephant likes to paint with his trunk.

Let's learn more about these talented animals and the creative work they do.

CHAPTER ONE

FROM TREES TO SKIS

In 1978, a **hurricane** brought wind and rain to Sanford, Florida. The wind knocked down trees and street signs. The rain flooded streets and basements. When the storm was over, Chuck and Lou Ann Best heard from one of their friends. The friend had found a baby squirrel. The squirrel had fallen from its nest at the top of a tree.

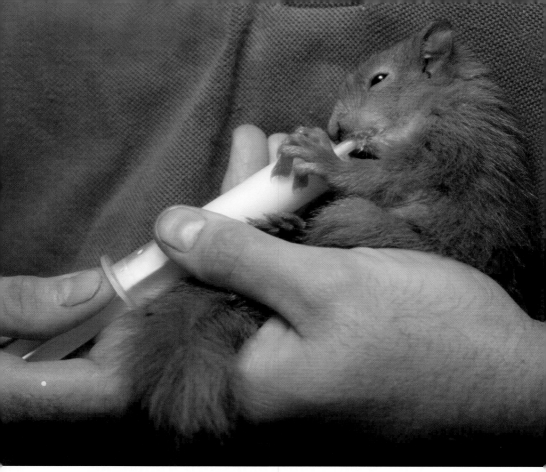

At birth, a baby squirrel weighs about 1 ounce (28 grams) and is about 1 inch (2.5 centimeters) long.

Chuck and Lou Ann took in the squirrel. They fed her and comforted her. After a few days, the squirrel began to get better. She greeted the Bests with friendly chirps.

The squirrel loved her new home. She ran from room to room. Sometimes she knocked things over. She especially liked to play games with the plants in the house. She attacked the plants and pulled off the leaves. Soon, nothing was left but twigs. Chuck and Lou Ann decided to call their new pet Twiggy.

Chuck and Lou Ann knew that Twiggy misbehaved because she was bored. What she needed was a hobby. Chuck had an idea. He and Lou Ann loved to water-ski. Maybe their new family member would also enjoy water-skiing.

Chuck and Lou Ann decided to find out. They gathered a large supply of nuts. They made a pair of **miniature** (MIN-ee-uh-chur) water skis and a tiny life jacket. Then, they fastened Twiggy to a remote-controlled toy boat and put her in the pool in their yard.

Each time Twiggy went around the pool,

she got a treat. Soon Twiggy was water skiing for thirty minutes at a time. It was clear she was having fun!

People were amazed to see a squirrel on water skis. Twiggy performed at hundreds of boat shows. Soon she became famous, especially after she appeared as a guest on television shows.

Twiggy learned to balance on water skis.

Twiggy rides inside the boat this time.

Twiggy holds on tight!

Lou Ann Best has taken in other
abandoned squirrels. Some were returned to
the wild when they were strong enough.
Others were trained to water ski. These
squirrels took Twiggy's place after she got too
old to perform. All of Lou Ann's water-skiing
squirrels have been named Twiggy.

Today's Twiggy has her own room with wall-to-wall **mulch**. Logs and tree branches are the furniture. Although she could eat in her own room, she prefers to dine on the kitchen counter. She has oatmeal with milk, butter, and sugar for breakfast. Cooked corn and potatoes are her favorite dinner. Twiggy snacks on pistachios (pi-STASH-ee-ohs), cashews, and sunflower seeds.

Twiggy is the star performer at about twenty boat shows every year. She travels to each show in a fancy motor home. No other squirrel has a more exciting life than Twiggy!

CHAPTER TWO

TOP DOGS

The stars of this chapter are two talented dogs. One dog is an artist. The other is an actor. The artist is a **pedigreed** dog that has always known love. Her name is Tillamook Cheddar. The actor is a mixed-breed that started life in an **animal shelter**. His name is Tracker.

TILLAMOOK CHEDDAR

Tillamook Cheddar lives with Bowman Hastie, her owner. She is called Tillie for short.

Sometimes Tillie uses her teeth to make designs.

Tillie loves to eat cheese. She is named after her favorite brand of cheese, Tillamook Cheddar.

Tillie made her first work of art when she was six months old. One day, Bowman was working at home. He left his writing pad on his desk and went to get a snack. When he returned, Tillie was scratching with her paws at his writing pad. The marks she made on the paper formed a design, or pattern.

Bowman wondered how Tillie's art would look in color. He tacked a piece of transfer paper to a white sheet of cardboard. Transfer paper is white on one side. The other side has a color coating. Bowman put the paper in front of Tillie. Scratch, scratch, scratch went Tillie. When Tillie was finished, Bowman removed the transfer paper. Underneath, there was a colorful painting. Tillie had made it all by herself! Bowman rewarded Tillie with a piece of her favorite cheese.

Tillie and Bowman

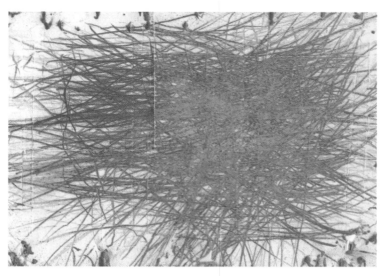

A piece of Tillie's art

Since that day, Tillie has made hundreds of paintings. The paintings have been shown at art shows all over the country. Some have sold for as much as 300 dollars. Tilly even has her own website. That's not bad for a little dog that loves to scratch!

Tillie with one of her works

TRACKER

Tracker is a movie star dog. No one knows where he came from. He was abandoned when he was a puppy. Luckily, someone rescued him and brought him to an animal shelter. The **caregivers** there fed him with a bottle and gave him lots of love.

Tracker might be part collie or part German shepherd. No one knows for sure. Some things are certain, though. He is very handsome. He is also very smart and friendly. One day, Anne Gordon, an animal trainer, visited the shelter. She spotted Tracker at once. There was something special about the friendly dog

Tracker with Anne

Tracker is on the set of his first movie.

with one floppy ear. Anne decided to bring
him home with her.

When Tracker was full-grown, Anne took
him to work with her. Tracker liked to
watch the other dogs pose for photos and
act in movies. The bright lights and noise
did not bother him.

Anne began training Tracker to become
an actor. He was a quick learner. Anne
taught him the hand signal for "sit" and
other commands that animal actors have to
know. Then she made a video of Tracker

performing all of his tricks. She made copies of the videos. She sent them to people who make movies and television shows. Soon, Tracker had his first job, a television commercial.

Tracker's part was easy. He had to lie down, then look surprised, as if something exciting had just happened. Anne gave the signal. Tracker sat up and perked up his ears. He performed his part perfectly. Everyone said he was a natural.

When Tracker was two years old, he got his first part in a movie. Tracker's **co-stars** in the movie were **chimpanzees**. The trainers for the chimps wondered if all the animals

Tracker plays with a chimpanzee named Louie.

Tracker with Corey Sener, lead actor
in *Summer of the Monkeys*

would get along. They did not have to
worry. When Tracker saw the chimpanzees,
he wagged his tail and trotted up to them to
make friends. The dog and the chimps had
fun chasing each other around the **set**.

Soon it was time to film the first **scene**.
Tracker's job was to act fierce and chase the
chimps away. Anne gave the signal. Tracker
growled. The chimps ran away. Everyone
was impressed. Tracker thought nothing of
it. After all, that's what good actors do.

CHAPTER THREE

A FINE ANIMAL GORILLA

Koko is a gorilla. She was born at the San Francisco Zoo in California. When Koko was six months old, she became very sick. Koko's caregivers were afraid she would die. Once she got better, Koko needed someone to take care of her full time. Doctor Penny Patterson, a scientist who studies gorillas, got the job.

Koko as a baby with Penny

Penny fed Koko with a bottle. She cuddled and played with her, too. Penny taught Koko **sign language** (sine LANG-gwij). That was many years ago. Now Koko knows over 1,000 signs and understands more than 2,000 spoken words.

Koko likes to look at pictures in books. Her favorite book is *The Three Little Kittens*. When she is given pens and paper, Koko likes to pretend to write her own books.

Penny has taught Koko over 1,000 signs.

Koko enjoys drawing and painting pictures, too. Sometimes Koko paints what she sees. Other times she uses her imagination. Whenever Koko wants to paint, her caregivers set up canvases, pots of paint, and paintbrushes.

One day, a caregiver rescued a baby blue jay that had fallen from its nest. Koko fed the blue

Koko likes to paint.

jay. She named it Tongue because the bird had such a big tongue. After Tongue had left, Koko painted a picture of the bird. She added special touches that made the painting her own. Splashes of yellow and red paint in the background make the blue bird stand out. Koko also painted a picture of her pet cat. She used black for the cat's body and tan for her eyes. She even painted her pet's green toy.

Koko with her pet cat

Michael, Koko's friend

Koko isn't the only gorilla that paints. Michael, Koko's close friend, also painted. In fact, many people considered Michael the more talented artist. Michael painted a picture of Apple, his black and white dog. Like Koko, he painted his pet from memory. He used white and black paint, even though he had many other colors to choose from.

When their paintings were finished, Koko and Michael named them. Once Koko painted a pink heart and named it *Love*.

Another time, Michael painted a big bunch of flowers. He called it *Stink Gorilla More*. For the gorillas, the sign "stink" means flowers as well as smell.

Stink Gorilla More **by Michael**

Lately, Koko's life has been busier than ever. She just starred in a movie about her life. She also made her first **compact disc**, or **CD**. It's called *Fine Animal Gorilla*. The **lyrics** (LIHR-iks) are based on signed talks she has had with her caregivers.

Koko told her caregivers the words she wanted used on the CD. For example, the words *Would I lie?* appeared on one of the songs. When Koko heard it, she signed the word *Shame!* Koko knows that lying is wrong. She did not want the words in her song, so they were changed.

These are the words to one of the songs:

Dr. Penny found me when I was just a baby.
Took me under her wing, she's such a pretty lady.
And in a short time she taught me how to sign.
She taught me how to paint cause she's so fine.
And I am Fine Animal Gorilla.

Fine Animal Gorilla is Koko's name for herself. Most people would agree that these words describe her just right.

CHAPTER FOUR

TRUNKS FULL OF TALENT

When Ruby came to the Phoenix Zoo in Arizona, she was the only elephant. Tawny Carlson, her caregiver, wanted to keep Ruby busy. She noticed that Ruby often made marks in the sand with her trunk. She seemed to like making these doodles. Tawny decided to teach Ruby how to paint.

Tawny gave Ruby a brush. She taught Ruby how to rub the brush against a piece of cardboard.

Ruby

A painting by Ruby

Each time Ruby did this, Tawny gave her a treat. Next, Tawny dipped the brush in paint. Ruby rubbed the brush against the cardboard. She was painting!

Ruby became famous. So did her paintings. Some of them have sold for as much as 5,000 dollars.

Ruby wasn't the only elephant that painted. Siri, an elephant that lived at the Burnet Zoo in Syracuse, New York, was a fine painter, too. Once, Siri's caregivers sent her paintings to a famous artist. They did not tell the artist that Siri was an elephant. The painter sent back this reply: "The artist who created the paintings has a lot of talent." Imagine the painter's surprise when he found out the artist was an elephant!

33

Like Ruby, Siri lived in a zoo. Most elephants live in the wild, though. In the forests of Asia and Africa, people have been clearing the land to build roads and houses. When they do this, they destroy the elephants' **habitats**. Without enough food to eat, many of these animals starve to death. One hundred years ago, there were 100,000 elephants in **Thailand** (TYE-land). Today, there are less than 4,000.

Vitaly Komar   Alex Melamid

Elephants painting on easels

Vitaly Komar and Alex Melamid are artists who want to help elephants. They decided to start an art school for elephants. The school is in Thailand. It is called the Asian Elephant Art and **Conservation** (kon-sur-VAY-shuhn) Project. At the school, large pieces of paper are pinned to easels.

There are about 40,000 muscles in an elephant's trunk.

The elephants are taught to hold the paintbrushes in the tips of their trunks. The elephants learn quickly. In the wild, elephants hold sticks the same way. They use the sticks to scratch themselves or to draw lines in the dirt.

Now the elephants are ready to paint! An elephant's **mahout** (ma-HOOT), or elephant trainer, dips the brush in some paint and offers it to the elephant. If the elephant likes the color, it will take the brush and begin painting. If the elephant doesn't like the color, it will refuse the brush. Then the mahout must try another color.

A painting by Bok Bak

At first, the mahouts guide the elephants' trunks over the canvas. Soon, the elephants get the idea and begin making their own designs.

After the elephants had been painting for a short time, Vitaly and Alex noticed something. Like human artists, each elephant had its own style. Most people could tell who the artist was just by looking at the painting. When painting, Tadpole chooses bright, strong colors. Add's paintings are full of curves and circles. Luuk Khang uses pastel colors to paint straight up-and-down lines.

These elephants are learning how to paint.

Richard Lair

Richard Lair also cares about elephants. He has started an elephant **orchestra** (OR-kuh-struh) at the Thai (TYE) Elephant Conservation Center. The orchestra raises money to help elephants. Richard built sturdy musical instruments that are the right size for the elephant players. The instruments are similar to ones played by people in Thailand.

Pratida plays the gongs. The gongs are made of cooking bowls that are attached to a wooden board. Add plays the renat, a kind of xylophone (ZYE-luh-fone), and Mae Kawt bangs a cymbal.

Every orchestra needs a conductor and this elephant band has one. His name is David Soldier. After David lines up the elephants, the mahouts give them their cue to begin. As the elephants play their instruments, they move their bodies. They flap their ears and swish their tails. Sometimes, they raise their trunks and trumpet.

David has put together a CD of the elephant's music. A music writer who listened to the CD was impressed. He wrote

The elephant orchestra

Richard conducts the orchestra.

that if you didn't know the musicians were elephants, you would think they were people.

Visitors pay to come to the park. They like to watch the elephants paint and perform on their instruments. Many people buy the elephants' paintings and their CDs. The money from both these projects is used to protect elephant habitats. Best of all, the elephants seem to be enjoying themselves.

GLOSSARY

abandoned left or given up completely

animal shelter a place that keeps unwanted animals

caregiver someone who cares for a person or other animal

chimpanzee a small ape that lives in trees

compact disc (CD) a round, flat object that holds recorded music

conservation (kon-sur-VAY-shuhn) the protection of Earth and its natural resources

co-star another actor in a movie

habitat the place where an animal or plant naturally lives or grows

hurricane a storm with strong winds

lyrics (LIHR-iks) the words to a song

mahout (ma-HOOT) an elephant trainer

miniature (MIN-ee-uh-chur) smaller than the usual size

mulch bits of plant material used as a covering

orchestra (OR-kuh-struh) a group that plays music together

pedigreed an animal whose parents were of the same type or breed

scene a part of a movie

set the place where a movie is filmed

sign language (sine LANG-gwij) a language that uses hand signs to communicate

talent a natural ability or skill

Thailand (TYE-land) a country in Southeast Asia

FIND OUT MORE

From Trees to Skis
www.squirrels.org
If you want to learn more about squirrels, visit this website.

Top Dogs
http://tillamookcheddar.com
Visit Tillie and see some of her scratch paintings.

A Fine Animal Gorilla
www.koko.org
Koko's website has a section just for kids. While you are there, become a member of Koko's fan club.

Trunks Full of Talent
www.artbyelephants.com
Meet the elephants from the Thai Conservation Center.

More Books to Read

Ruby: The Story of a Painting Pachyderm by Dick George, Bantam Doubleday Dell Books for Young Readers, 1995

Koko-Love!: Conversations with a Talking Gorilla by Francine Patterson, Penguin Putnam Books for Young Readers, 1999

Squirrels by Brian Wildsmith, Oxford University Press, 1984

INDEX

PHOTO CREDITS

MEET THE AUTHOR

The author of more than 200 picture books, Mary Packard has been writing for children for as long as she can remember. She lives in Northport, New York, with her husband, Dave, and her dog and cat, Linus and Fraggle.

Her love for animals began as a little girl when she would visit her grandparents' farm in Oklahoma each summer. There, she would feed the chicks, help milk the cows, and play with the baby goats. It was from her grandfather that she learned to respect all living things and to understand how much animals and humans depend upon one another.

Packard has always lived with a cat and dog or two. One of them, a Hungarian sheepdog named Josh, liked to sing when her daughters practiced piano. Like most animals, all of her pets have been gifted with a talent for friendship.